TAIWAN TRAVEL GUIDE 2024

Navigating Taipei & Beyond - Embark on an Epic Journey through the Heart of Taiwan's Natural Beauty and Culture

Adeline Palmerstone

TABLE OF CONTENTS

INTRODUCTION

Taiwan is a wonderful destination to visit since it is located in the heart of East Asia. It has a little bit of everything, from bustling cities to serene natural areas. Consider yourself in a place where old traditions and new ideas coexist, such as ancient temples and modern skyscrapers. Taiwan is a paradise waiting to be discovered, and I'm here to help you get there with the "Taiwan Explorer's Guide: From Taipei to Beyond."

Close your eyes and imagine yourself trekking through the breathtaking Taroko Gorge. It's like wandering amid massive marble walls that reach almost to the sky. Consider strolling through Jiufen's small lanes, where lanterns softly wave in the air and convey stories from the past. And don't get us started on the cuisine! With all of the hot street cuisine and unusual flavors, Taiwanese night markets are like a delectable dream. You might even imagine yourself in front of majestic temples with the aroma of incense filling the air.

Taiwan is like a surprise package. Taipei is a large and busy city with lofty skyscrapers and plenty to do. However, if you drive a little farther, you'll find Alishan's tranquil forests and Tainan's rich culture. Kenting is also a tropical paradise for beach lovers.

Regardless of what sort of explorer you are - assuming you love experience, history, food, or simply unwinding - Taiwan has something uniquely amazing for you.

This journey will begin in Taipei, Taiwan's dynamic capital. Then we'll visit the island's secret nooks, areas that few people know about. You'll learn how to navigate Taiwan's excellent public transit system. In addition, I'll give insider insights from the locals and expose you to Taiwan's distinct culture. This book will be your closest friend while you tour Taiwan, from practical recommendations to must-see attractions.

So be ready for an incredible journey! Taiwan is brimming with gems just waiting to be discovered. "Taiwan Explorer's Guide: From Taipei to Beyond" will help you explore all the mysteries of this amazing location, from Taipei to the farthest parts of this lovely island. You're about to go on a once-in-a-lifetime adventure and fall in love with Taiwan. Let the journey begin!

Overview of Key Information about Taiwan

Taiwan, formally known as the Republic of China (ROC), is an East Asian island republic. Here is a summary of important Taiwan information:

Geography:

Ø To the east of China, to the south of Japan, and to the north of the Philippines is Taiwan, which is in the western Pacific Ocean.

Ø The majority of Taiwan's territory is comprised of the largest island, Taiwan. It is 144 kilometers (89 miles) wide and approximately 394 kilometers (245 miles) long.

Ø Taiwan likewise incorporates a few more modest islands, the most eminent of which are Penghu (the Pescadores), Kinmen (Quemoy), and Matsu.

Population:

Ø   Starting around my last information update, Taiwan had a populace of around 23 million individuals.

Ø Taipei is Taiwan's largest and capital city, and it is in the north of the island.

Government:

Ø   Taiwan is a democratic republic that has a political system with multiple parties.

Ø A presidential system with a separation of powers includes a President, a Legislative Yuan (parliament), and an independent judiciary as the foundation of the government.

Ø There are several political parties in the political landscape, with the two major parties being the Kuomintang (KMT) and the Democratic Progressive Party (DPP).

History:

Ø Taiwan has a long and complicated history, with indigenous people having settled there for thousands of years.

Ø The island was colonized by the Dutch in the seventeenth hundred years, trailed by the Ming Administration and Qing traditional rule. Following the First Sino-Japanese War, Taiwan was handed over to Japan in 1895.

Ø After The Second World War, Taiwan was put under the managerial control of the Republic of China (ROC) government, which withdrew to the island after losing the Chinese Civil War to the Chinese Communist Party (CCP) in the central area.

Ø Taiwan transitioned to democracy in the late 20th century after a time of authoritarian rule under the ROC.

Ø The People's Republic of China (PRC) claims Taiwan as a province and has not ruled out the use of force to reunite it with the mainland, making Taiwan's political status a complicated and contentious issue today. Taiwan, then again, works as a sovereign state with its administration, military, and constitution.

Economy:

Ø   Taiwan has a profoundly evolved and trade-focused economy.

Ø It is well-known for its advanced technology sector, which includes the production of semiconductors, an essential component of global electronics supply chains.

Ø Other key businesses incorporate manufacturing, money, and administration.

Culture:

Ø The indigenous, Chinese, Japanese, and Western influences are all present in Taiwanese culture.

Ø Although Taiwanese Hokkien (Min Nan) and indigenous languages are also spoken, Mandarin Chinese is the official language.

Ø The culture is characterized not only by its distinctive traditions and customs but also by

traditional Chinese festivals like the Lunar New
Year.

Ø With dishes like beef noodle soup, xiao long bao
(soup dumplings), and a wide range of street
foods, Taiwanese cuisine is both diverse and
well-known.

Tourism:

Ø Taiwan is a famous traveling location known for
its normal magnificence, including picturesque
regions like Taroko Crevasse, Sun Moon Lake,
and Alishan.

Ø Taipei, the capital, provides a vibrant urban
experience with night markets, cultural sites, and
attractions like Taipei 101.

Ø Temples, historical sites, and traditional
performances are just a few of Taiwan's many
attractions for tourists.

Now I've given you the overview of the important
information you need to have at your fingertips to
arm yourself with knowledge of the location you

wish to visit, let's get to the meat of this guide.

CHAPTER 1: INTRODUCTION TO THE JOURNEY

My First Glimpse of Taiwan

Hey there, fellow explorer! I'm thrilled to have you join me on this adventure as we embark on a journey through the enchanting island of Taiwan. Before we dive into the nitty-gritty details, let me take you back to my very first glimpse of this incredible destination.

It all began with a single glimpse, a fleeting moment as my plane descended towards Taoyuan International Airport. The island of Taiwan, nestled in the heart of East Asia, emerged from beneath the clouds, revealing its rugged coastlines, lush mountains, and the gleaming skyline of Taipei. That first sight was a promise of adventure, an invitation to explore a land where tradition dances with modernity, where natural beauty beckons at every corner, and where every day holds the potential for discoveries.

At that moment, I felt a rush of excitement and curiosity. Taiwan had always been a destination that piqued my interest, but as the aircraft touched down on the runway, I realized that this trip was going to be different. It was going to be extraordinary.

I arrived at Taoyuan International Airport (TPE) in Taipei, Taiwan, on a hot and humid day on September 5th. I was excited to start my trip, but I was also a little bit nervous. I had never been to Taiwan before, and I didn't speak any Mandarin Chinese.

I followed the signs to the arrivals hall and went through immigration and customs. Once I had my passport stamped, I headed to the taxi stand. I took a taxi to my hostel [Royal Rose Hotel Ximen], which was located in the Ximending district of Taipei.

The taxi ride took about 30 minutes, and it cost me around NT$200. When I arrived at the hostel, I checked in and was given a key to my room. I was tired from my flight, so I decided to take a nap before exploring the city.

My hotel apartment was double-standard and clean. It had a king-size bed, and other luxurious fittings, and of course, it was more like a 3-star [winks]. The whole hotel apartment was extravagantly cozy with its kitchen. I unpacked my things and then took a nap. After my nap, I went out to explore the Ximending district. It was a lively and vibrant area with a lot of shops, restaurants, and bars. I wandered around for a while, taking in the sights and sounds. I eventually found a small restaurant and had dinner.

After dinner, I went back to my hostel and called it a night. I was exhausted from my long day of travel, but I was also excited to start exploring Taiwan the next day.

Here are some of the things I experienced on my arrival from the airport to the hostel:

- ·   I experienced the hustle and bustle of a busy airport.
- ·   I interacted with people who spoke a different language than me.
- · I learned how to use public transportation in a new city.
- ·   I stayed in a hostel with other travelers from all over the world.

- · I explored a new neighborhood and tried new foods.

Why Taiwan? The Allure of the Island

Now, you might be wondering, "Why Taiwan?" What makes this island stand out among the many travel destinations around the world? Well, my friend, that's what we're about to explore.

Taiwan is like a hidden gem waiting to be discovered. It's an island nation that packs a punch when it comes to diversity and charm. Here are a few reasons why Taiwan had me hooked from the start:

1. A Land of Contrasts: Taiwan seamlessly blends tradition and modernity. In one moment, you can find yourself wandering through ancient temples steeped in history, and in the next, you're exploring futuristic skyscrapers in bustling Taipei.

2. Culinary Paradise: If you're a food enthusiast like me, Taiwan is a dream come true. The island's street food culture is legendary, with tantalizing dishes like Xiaolongbao (soup dumplings), stinky tofu, and the world-famous bubble tea. Your taste buds are in for a treat!

3. Natural Beauty: Taiwan is a playground for nature lovers. From the dramatic landscapes of Taroko Gorge to the serene beauty of Sun Moon Lake and the lush forests of Alishan, there's a world of outdoor adventures waiting for you.

4. Warm Hospitality: The people of Taiwan are incredibly welcoming. Whether you're chatting with a street food vendor, seeking directions, or engaging in a cultural exchange, you'll find that the locals are friendly and eager to share their culture with you.

5. Adventure Awaits: Whether you're into hiking, cycling, water sports, or simply exploring new horizons, Taiwan offers a wide range of activities for adventure seekers.

So, my fellow traveler, if you're looking for a destination that combines the thrill of exploration with the comforts of modern travel, Taiwan is the place to be. Together, we'll uncover the secrets of this remarkable island, and I'll share with you all the tips, insights, and memories that made my trip to Taipei and beyond an unforgettable experience.

Now that you have a taste of what Taiwan has in store, let's embark on this journey together. In the chapters that follow, we'll delve deeper into the planning, the adventures, the culinary delights, the cultural discoveries, and everything in between. Get ready to pack your bags, ignite your wanderlust, and set off on an incredible Taiwan adventure!

My name is **Adeline Palmerstone**, Welcome to Taiwan!

CHAPTER 2: PREPARING FOR YOUR TAIWAN ADVENTURE

Planning Your Trip

Making plans for any trip, whether to a known or completely strange destination, is very pertinent to getting yourself organized and prepared to have a wonderful experience. As such, let's get started on the fun process of organizing your Taiwan journey! Making a blueprint for your trip is what planning is all about, and it can be a lot of fun. Here's what you should know:

Choosing the Right Time

First, consider when you want to visit Taiwan. Throughout the year, the island has varied attractions. Spring (March to May) boasts lovely cherry blossoms and nice weather, while fall (September to November) provides warm temperatures and vibrant leaves. Summer (June to August) can be hot and humid, but winter (December to February) is milder but less crowded.

To explain further, Taiwan is best visited in the spring (March to May) or fall (September to November). During these months, the weather is moderate and bright, making it ideal for outdoor activities.

Taiwan, on the other hand, is a lovely island all year. If you want to avoid crowds, visit during the winter (December to February). The temperature is colder during this time of year, but there is still much to see and do.

Factors to Look Into Before Traveling to Taiwan

Weather: Taiwan has moderate weather all year, but the ideal time to come is in the spring or fall when the weather is bright and sunny.

Festivals: Taiwan hosts several festivals throughout the year, including the Lantern Festival in February, the Dragon Boat Festival in June, and the Mid-Autumn Festival in September.

Peak Season: The summer (June to August) and holiday seasons (around Christmas and New Year) are the busiest times for tourism in Taiwan. It is advised to avoid visiting during these hours if you wish to avoid crowds.

Off-Season: Taiwan's off-seasons for tourism include winter (December to February) and rainy season (May to July). You can get more affordable rates on flights and hotels during certain periods.

In a nutshell, the best time to visit Taiwan is determined by your unique tastes and interests. If you want to avoid crowds and enjoy the nicest weather, spring and fall are the ideal times to visit. If you want to experience Taiwanese festivals, you should come during the summer or vacations. If you want to save money on your holiday, the winter or rainy season may be an excellent choice.

Duration of Stay

Determine how long you will be in Taiwan. Some visitors stay for a week, while others stay for a month or more. Your itinerary will be influenced by the length of your vacation.

Knowing how long you intend to stay in Taiwan is crucial to your preparation. It will help you calculate your potential expenditures and budget properly in order not to be taken unawares or stranded in a strange land trying to find your way back home.

My visit to Taiwan was well planned because I decided that I would only spend 2 weeks [14 days], and that was it!

Creating an Itinerary

Now comes the exciting part: route planning! Ensure you plan what you want to see and do – the activities you may likely want to get involved in. Do you wish to visit enchanting cities, go on mountain hikes, relax on beaches, or do all of the above? Make a rundown of locations you desire to pay a visit and activities you wish to participate in. This will assist you in developing a preliminary itinerary.

Accommodation

Begin searching at lodging choices. Taiwan has a broad selection of accommodations, from expensive hotels to comfortable guesthouses and budget-friendly hostels. Consider your budget and travel preferences. Booking.com and Airbnb are excellent resources for locating somewhere to stay.

You don't need to live lavishly when deciding your accommodation needs. I booked a double-standard room in the Ximending district of Taipei, the capital city of Taiwan. All I wanted was comfort and serenity. You are also free to have as much fun as possible! Head over to Booking.com and browse through affordable or extravagant hotels that would suit your needs. You may want to have the time of your life by opting for a 5-star hotel suite, it's still cool! The aim is to enjoy your vacation in Taiwan to the fullest.

Taiwan has a wide range of housing alternatives, from inexpensive hostels to luxury hotels. Here are some of Taiwan's most popular forms of lodging:

Hostels: Hostels are an excellent choice for budget tourists. They have both shared and private dorms.

Hotels: Hotels provide a wide range of accommodation kinds, from regular rooms to suites.

Bed & Breakfasts: Bed and breakfasts provide a more intimate setting. Breakfast is usually included in the price.

Guesthouses: Guesthouses are comparable to bed and breakfasts, however they usually have lower prices.

Homestays: Homestays are an excellent method to learn about Taiwanese culture. You will live with an indigenous family and acquire knowledge about their culture.

The cost of lodging in Taiwan varies based on the kind of facility and its location. Hostels are a more cost-effective choice, with hostel beds costing around NT$500 per night. Hotels begin at around NT$1,000 per night, while bed and breakfasts range at about NT$1,500 per night. Guesthouses and homestays are usually even cheaper.

When selecting accommodations in Taiwan, keep your budget, travel style, and interests in mind. Hostels are an excellent choice for those on a tight budget. Hotels are an excellent option if you want a more luxurious experience. A homestay is also an excellent way to immerse yourself in Taiwanese culture.

Recommended Accommodations to Go for In Taiwan

Depending on your budget and interests, these are some of the best locations to stay in Taiwan:

Budget: I suggest lodging in a hostel in Taipei or Kaohsiung for economic tourists. These cities have a lot of decent hostels, which are a fantastic way to get acquainted with others who are visiting.

Mid-Range: I recommend lodging at a hotel in Taipei or Taichung for an inexpensive choice. These cities have a lot of nice hotels with a range of services and amenities to choose from.

Luxury: I propose staying at a hotel in Hualien or Kenting for a luxury vacation. These cities are home to some of Taiwan's top hotels, and they provide breathtaking views of the island's natural splendor.

Transportation

What are your plans for transportation? Taiwan's public transportation system is good, with buses, trains, and the Taipei Metro. The High-Speed Rail (HSR) swiftly links major cities. In some spots, you may even hire a scooter. Consider what will work most effectively for your trip arrangements.

Taiwan's most prevalent type of transportation is

Public Transportation: Taiwan has an advanced public transportation infrastructure that makes getting about the island simple. The Taipei Metro is the most convenient method to move about the city. Buses, taxis, and rental automobiles are also accessible.

Taxis: Taxis are a comfortable mode of transportation, but they may be costly. The cost begins at NT$70 and increases with the distance covered.

Buses: Buses are an inexpensive and effective mode of transportation. The cost of the trip ranges from NT$15-25 for each ride.

Rental Car: If you intend to do a lot of chauffeuring, you should consider renting a car. Nevertheless, public transportation is also a great way to get around the island.

High-Speed Rail: The HSR is a quick and easy means to make trips between Taiwan's biggest cities.

Taipei, Kaohsiung, Taichung, and Taoyuan are all served by the railway.

Taiwan Tourist Shuttle: The Taiwan Tourist Shuttle is a bus service that links important Taiwanese tourist sites. The bus is a suitable and pleasant method to move about the island.

Your budget, time of day, and destination will all influence the best option of transportation for you. If you're on limited funds, public transportation is your best bet. If you are constrained on time, the HSR is the most efficient mode of transportation. A rental car is also an excellent alternative if you want to tour the island at your own pace.

Budget

It is critical to create a budget. Taiwan might be inexpensive, but expenditures can mount up. Budget for lodging, food, transportation, activities, and a little more for recollections and unforeseen costs.

Visa and Travel Documents

Let's get started on the paperwork you'll need to complete before your Taiwan trip:

Visa Requirements

You may require a visa to enter Taiwan, based on your country of citizenship. Most travelers can remain without a visa for up to 90 days. If you want to verify the criteria for your country, visit the Taiwan Bureau of Consular Affairs official website or reach out to the closest Taiwanese embassy or consulate.

Passport

Make sure your passport is valid for a minimum of six months above your intended flight date from Taiwan, and confirm it now to avoid unexpected events later!

Travel Insurance

Look into getting travel insurance that includes coverage for medical emergencies, trip cancellations flights, and misplaced bags. It's a safety net that can save your life in an emergency.

Packing Essentials

One of the essentials for planning your Taiwan trip properly is the necessary items you would need during your vacation, and these things are compulsory for your comfort. Let's look at a few of them:

Clothing

The weather in Taiwan fluctuates, so pack appropriately. Light, breathable clothing is ideal for the summer months, but have a light jacket on hand for cooler evenings. Bring layers, especially a heavy jacket, in the cold. Walking shoes that are cozy are essential for sightseeing.

Electronics

Taiwan's electrical connections are Type A and Type B, therefore carry an all-purpose adaptor if your gadgets have different adapters. Remember to bring your phone, camera, and chargers!

Medications

Ensure that you have sufficient pharmaceutical-prescribed medications to last the duration of your vacation. It's also an excellent precaution to keep a compact first-aid kit on hand, complete with bandages and pain supplements.

Travel Documents

Store your passport, visa (if necessary), travel insurance information, and a duplicate of your travel schedule in a safe, readily obtainable spot.

Money

Have some Taiwanese New Taiwan Dollars (TWD) in cash for little purchases. In cities, credit cards are usually permitted while cash is useful in more rural destinations.

Toiletries

While toiletries are readily available in Taiwan, it is an excellent plan to pack necessities such as toothpaste, a toothbrush, and any special items you enjoy.

Keep in mind that packing is an individual's decision. Pack only what you like traveling with, and allow some room for keepsakes you might find along the road. Prepare for your Taiwan excursion now that you've mastered the fundamentals of trip preparation.

CHAPTER 3: ARRIVING IN TAIPEI – YOUR GATEWAY TO TAIWAN

Touching Down at Taoyuan International Airport

As you step off your plane and into Taoyuan International Airport, the warm environment and excellent services will make you feel right at home. This sophisticated airport serves as Taiwan's principal international gateway and is well-known for its neat and orderly appearance.

Immigration and Customs

Your airport adventure starts with immigration and customs. Prepare your passport, visa (if necessary), and customs declaration document for examination. Because of the adequately educated team, the entire procedure is usually quick and painless.

Baggage Claim

Once you have cleared customs, proceed to the baggage claim department to retrieve your bags. The luggage recovery system at Taoyuan Airport is well-known for its dependability, so you are likely to have a pleasant experience.

Currency Exchange and ATMs

If you require some local currency (New Taiwan Dollars or TWD), the airport has currency exchange counters and ATMs. It's recommended to have some cash with you, particularly if you want to take public transit or taxis upon arrival.

Dining Options

If your flight has made you hungry, you're fortunate. Taoyuan Airport offers a wide range of eating selections, from traditional Taiwanese dishes to international cuisine. It's an incredible chance to try Taiwanese cuisine for the first time.

Transportation to Taipei

After you've cleared customs, you're ready to go to the busy capital city of Taipei. There are various viable options:

Airport Shuttle: Go for the airport shuttle bus service, which provides pleasant and air-conditioned transportation to many sites across Taipei. The airport's signpost will direct you to the bus terminal.

Taoyuan Airport MRT: Take advantage of the Taoyuan Airport Mass Rapid Transit (MRT) route as a quick and effective mode of transportation. It will take about 35-40 minutes to get to Taipei Main Station. Around the airport, look for MRT signage.

Taxis: Taxis are also widely accessible at the airport. They are an efficient option, particularly in case you're carrying a lot of luggage or are traveling in the company of others. With respect to traffic, the trip to Taipei will take between 40 and 50 minutes.

Navigating Taipei's Efficient Transportation

Now that you've arrived in Taipei, let's speak about getting around and seeing the city's various attractions. Taipei has a well-organized and easy-to-use public transit system that's designed to make it simple for tourists to get around the city.

Taipei Metro (MRT): The Taipei Metro, also known as the MRT, is the city's transportation network's solid base. It's neat, secure, and quite handy. The system spans the majority of the city and provides convenient access to famous places such as major attractions for tourists, commercial areas, and cultural centers.

Ticketing: At MRT stations, you may buy single-journey tickets or prepaid EasyCards. The EasyCard is a smart card with a chip that lets you use the MRT framework, pay for bus journeys, and make payments at grocery stores.

MRT: MRT stations are well-marked, with legible labeling in both English and Chinese. Maps and station descriptions can be accessed readily, enabling route planning a breeze.

Accessibility: The MRT system is constructed with stairs, elevators, and special spaces aboard trains in mind for travelers with impairments.

Taipei City Buses: Besides having access to the MRT, Taipei has a vast bus network. These are especially useful for getting to places that are not easy to access by metro. The majority of bus routes are clearly signposted, and automated fare payment with your EasyCard is frequent.

Bus Stops: Look for bus stops that have directions. Bus stations frequently include computerized screens that show predicted arrival times.

Fare Payment: As previously stated, using an EasyCard is the most convenient way to make payments for bus trips. You may also use precise change but have small denominations on hand.

Walking: Taipei is a pedestrian-friendly city, and walking is generally the easiest way to get about. Many areas and places of interest are within walking distance of one another, and while you meander across the city, you'll have the opportunity to uncover hidden jewels, street food sellers, and picturesque lanes.

Let's pause for a moment and look into the details of EasyCard [in other words EasyCard Taiwan]. If you must enjoy hassle-free financial transactions in Taiwan in the course of your vacation, you must come to terms with getting acquainted with the EasyCard payment system.

EasyCard Taiwan

The EasyCard is a contactless smartcard that is frequently utilized within Taiwan to make payments for public transportation and other amenities. It is a handy and cashless mode of transportation that may also be used to make purchases at participating stores.

The EasyCard may be used at a variety of venues in Taiwan, including:

1. Taiwan's metro systems (Taipei, Taichung, Kaohsiung, and Taoyuan Airport MRT).

2. Trains from Taiwan Railway and High-Speed Rail.

3. Rental bicycle services such as YouBike in Taipei and T-Bike in Tainan.

4. City buses throughout the surrounding area.

5. Choose ferry services.

6. Taxis.

7. A diverse assortment of merchants, such as convenience stores, department stores, and supermarkets.

An EasyCard can be obtained from any of the locations listed below:

1. Vending machines that accept EasyCard.

2. Convenience shops (for example, 7-Eleven, FamilyMart, and Hi-Life).

3. Department shops (for example, Shin Kong Mitsukoshi, Sogo, and Far East Department Store).

Supermarkets (such as PX Mart, Carrefour, and Costco).

5. Visitor information centers.

6. Customer Service Center for EasyCard Corporation.

The EasyCard costs NT$500, which is around USD$16. This cost includes NT$400 in spending credit deposited onto the card, with the remaining NT$100 non-refundable. You may top up your EasyCard at the same locations where you bought it, as well as through vending machines and ticket dispensers in some situations.

When entering or departing a public transit station or making a purchase at a participating shop, just touch your EasyCard on the scanner. The amount of the fare or transaction will be automatically deducted from the card's balance.

If you happen to lose your EasyCard, you can notify the EasyCard Corporation, and they will deactivate the card while sending a replacement. Please keep in mind that any balance left on the lost card cannot be repaid.

Here are some extra details about EasyCards to be aware of:

1. Maximum Balance: An EasyCard can contain up to NT$10,000 in balance.

2. Card Lifespan: The card has a 5-year lifespan and may need to be changed after that.

3. Balance move: If necessary, you may move the balance from one EasyCard to another, which is useful if you lose your card but want to save your balance.

4. Parking Payment: In addition to paying for public transit and retail transactions, you may use your EasyCard to pay for parking at certain parking garages, providing additional variety and convenience.

Being armed with EasyCard knowledge is crucial for navigating your way through necessary financial commitments in Taiwan.

CHAPTER 4: TAIPEI DELIGHTS - TOURING TAIWAN'S CAPITAL CITY

Taipei 101: Iconic Skyscraper and Shopping Paradise

One of your first stops in the capital should be Taipei 101, a real icon of Taiwan's technology. This colossal skyscraper, reaching an astounding 508 meters (1,667 feet), was formerly the world's highest structure. Its one-of-a-kind architecture, inspired by bamboo, exemplifies Taiwan's dedication to mixing heritage with modernity.

The engineering marvel Taipei 101 features a one-of-a-kind design influenced by ancient Chinese pagodas and bamboo. It is more than simply a skyscraper; it represents Taiwan's creativity and aspiration. The 101 stories of the structure aren't simply for show; they signify the aspiration for expansion and wealth.

Observation Deck

A trip to Taipei 101 would be incomplete without a visit to the observation deck. The view from here is stunning, offering views of Taipei's expansive metropolis as well as the gorgeous bordering mountains. On a clear day, you could be able to see the distant shoreline.

Shopping Paradise

Taipei 101 is not only about height and vistas; it is also a retail wonderland. The building's lower levels are home to a plethora of upscale boutiques, foreign brands, and local retailers. Whether you're looking for luxurious apparel or distinctive Taiwanese souvenirs, Taipei 101 has you covered.

Dining with a View

When you've finished shopping, treat yourself to a cuisine treat at one of the tower's eateries. Dining with a vista that goes as far as the eye can see is simply spectacular.

Indulging in Taiwanese Street Food

Taiwan is a foodie's dream, and no trip to Taipei makes sense without experiencing Taiwanese street cuisine. The city's night markets are famed, offering a sensory overload of tastes and aromas.

Shilin Night Market

Shilin Night Market is one of Taipei's most well-known night marketplaces. A bewildering selection of street food sellers sell everything from stinky tofu and oyster omelets to bubble tea and freshly grilled seafood here. Try something different; Taiwanese street cuisine is renowned for its robust and varied tastes.

Raohe Night Market

Yet another must-see culinary location is Raohe Night Market. It's famous for its "black pepper bun," a delectable meat-filled pastry fried on a heated griddle. There's also a selection of classic snacks and sweets.

Ximending Street Food

Whilst touring the artistic scene in Ximending (which we'll get to in a minute), try some of the street food options. Ximending's street food scene is a feast for the senses, with everything from fiery hotpot to crunchy fried chicken.

Cultural Immersion at the National Palace Museum

The National Palace Museum is a must-see for anybody interested in Taiwan's rich cultural and historical past. This world-famous museum has a magnificent collection of Chinese art and antiquities, many of which were transferred to Taiwan during the Chinese Civil War.

Priceless Treasures

Ancient Chinese paintings, calligraphy, porcelain, jade, and uncommon documents from the past are among the museum's valuable collections. The Jadeite Cabbage, a tiny but detailed sculpture that is now a nationally recognized emblem of Taiwan, is one of its most notable sculptures.

Exhibits that are Interactive

The National Palace Museum has displays that are interactive as well as multimedia presentations that assist tourists in comprehending the rich past and cultural value of the relics. You'll learn about China's dynasty history while admiring the craftsmanship of these eternal gems.

Picturesque Grounds

Aside from the art and history, the museum is placed in a beautiful setting encompassed by lush gardens and gorgeous surroundings. A stroll around the beautiful grounds is a relaxing and mindful experience.

Exploring the Creative Scene in Ximending

Ximending, sometimes known as Taipei's "Harajuku," is a bustling and artistic area that attracts both locals and visitors. It's a hotspot for young people's culture, fashion, and entertainment.

Shopping and Boutiques

Ximending is well-known for its shopping options. There are stylish boutiques, offbeat streetwear shops, and multinational names. It's the ideal spot for trendy apparel, accessories, and one-of-a-kind souvenirs.

Street Performers

Street performers, musicians, and artists fill the streets of Ximending. It's typical to come across spontaneous concerts and exhibitions, which add to the dynamic mood of the region.

Cafes & Food Stalls

There are several cafes, food stalls, and restaurants in Ximending that serve a wide variety of gastronomic delicacies. Whether you're looking for a refreshing bubble tea, a substantial bowl of beef noodle soup, or a modern fusion cuisine, you're sure to find it here.

The Red House

The ancient Red House, a Western-style architecture building that today shelters an arts and crafts market, should not be missed. It's an excellent spot for visitors to discover and find one-of-a-kind handcrafted goods, artworks, and gifts.

CHAPTER 5: BEYOND TAIPEI – DAY TRIPS AND ADVENTURES

Now your vacation is getting to its climax! How about engaging in day trips and adventures into the hinterlands? That sounds like a great idea, right? Let's see what these locations have in store for us!

The Majestic Taroko Gorge

Brace is to be amazed as you travel through Taipei to the magnificent Taroko Gorge. This ecological treasure, located in Taroko National Park on Taiwan's east coast, exemplifies the island's stunning scenery.

Marble Marvel

Taroko Gorge is known as the "Marble Gorge" because of its stunning marble rocks that appear to rise indefinitely upward. The Liwu River has etched its way through these massive boulders over millennia, producing a truly breathtaking scene.

Scenic Trails

Taroko Gorge has something for everyone, whether or not you're a climbing aficionado or simply like going for a walk. There are several hiking paths for people of all skill levels. The Shakadang Trail, for example, provides an easy hike beside the crystal-clear waters of the Shakadang River, giving visitors a close-up glimpse of the gorge's natural grandeur.

Eternal Spring Shrine

A lovely shrine set on the side of a mountain, the Eternal Spring Shrine is a must-see. The shrine serves as a memorial to the remembrance of those who died while working on the Central Cross-Island Highway. The falling waterfall background to the monument adds to its tranquil charm.

Swallow Grotto

Don't miss Swallow Grotto, a portion of the valley famed for its high cliffs and Pacific swallow bird nests. It's an excellent location for photographs and admiring the natural world at its most stunning.

Tranquil Escape to Sun Moon Lake

Sun Moon Lake, located in the center of Taiwan, is a calm and lovely place that offers an idyllic respite from the hustle and bustle of daily life.

Breathtaking Scenery

Sun Moon Lake boasts some of Taiwan's most gorgeous views, enveloped by luxuriant woods and dominated by the high peaks of the Central Mountain Range. The lake's name comes from its unusual form, with one side symbolizing the sun and the other the moon.

Boat Rides

Taking a boat trip is the finest way to admire the lake's splendor. You may sail along the clear waterways, past temples, pagodas, and the Lalu Island Wildlife Reserve. Many guests enjoy the relaxing feeling of gliding around the lake.

Cycling and Hiking

If you enjoy being active, hire a bike to tour the picturesque lakeside riding lanes, or go on a hiking excursion in the neighboring hills. Trails such as the Ci'en Pagoda Trail provide breathtaking views.

Local Culture

Sun Moon Lake is also the residence of the Thao people, a native Taiwanese tribe. Cultural events and trips to the Thao Cultural Village might teach you about their culture and practices.

Alishan's Enchanted Forests

Alishan, a hilly location in central Taiwan, is known for its beautiful woods, old cypress trees, and exquisite dawn views.

Forest Bathing

The Alishan National Scenic Area is a nature lover's paradise. Walk amid the magnificent cypress forests, some of which are over 1,000 years old. The term "forest bathing" takes on a fresh significance here, since the tranquil environment is rejuvenating.

Sunrise at Zhushan

Alishan is well-known for its morning vistas, notably at Zhushan (Bamboo Mountain). You'll want to get up early and take a charming train journey to the observation balcony to see this spectacular show. The sun appears from behind the mountains, casting a warm and dreamy hue across the countryside.

Cherry Blossom Season

If the time you're there falls during the spring season, you're in for an unforgettable experience. The cherry blossoms of Alishan are revered across the country, and the cherry blossom season typically runs from late January to early February. The appearance of full-bloom cherry blossoms over a woodland setting is just lovely.

Fenqihu Old Street

While visiting Alishan, don't forget to stop at Fenqihu Old Street, an enchanting town with an intriguing past. Tea houses, gift stores, and restaurants fill the historic street. Try the Alishan tea, a local specialty.

These day trips and activities outside of Taipei entice them with their particular beauty and cultural relevance. Taroko Gorge, Sun Moon Lake, and Alishan provide glimpses into Taiwan's varied scenes from nature, which range from stunning gorges to calm lakes and old forests. Each place provides incredible adventures that will leave you with enduring memories of your Taiwan tour.

CHAPTER 6: TAIWAN'S CULINARY SCENE – A GASTRONOMIC ADVENTURE

Taiwan's culinary environment is a rich tapestry of tastes, and its night markets are the beating core of this cuisine culture. Exploring these crowded gourmet hotspots is a journey in and of itself.

Navigating Night Markets

Shilin Night Market in Taipei:

We've previously discussed Shilin Night Market, but it's worth mentioning again. The aroma of grilled meats, the sizzling of hot oil, and the merriment of residents and tourists alike foster an enticing ambiance here. Try some of the market's most popular foods, including oyster vermicelli, fresh fruit smoothies, and, of course, stinky tofu.

Raohe Night Market

Also in Taipei, Raohe Night Market provides an even more modest but just as fascinating cuisine trip. Keep in mind to get the pepper buns, pork rib soup, and a cup of herbal tea to refresh yourself. As you go through the market's small aisles, you'll come across a plethora of gastronomic wonders.

Fengjia Night Market

Fengjia Night Market in Taichung is a foodie's heaven. Takoyaki (octopus balls), grilled squid, and tall fruit-filled sweets are among the market's inventive street foods. It's a colorful atmosphere that encapsulates Taiwan's street food culture.

Keelung Night Market

If you happen to be located in northern Taiwan, you must stop by Keelung Night Market. It's famous for its seafood, with vendors selling anything from grilled squid to seafood porridge. Don't pass up the opportunity to enjoy the day's freshest catches.

Signature Dishes: From Beef Noodle Soup to Bubble Tea

Taiwan has a rich and diversified culinary tradition, including trademark dishes that have won recognition worldwide.

Beef Noodle Soup

Taiwan's national cuisine, beef noodle soup, is a hearty bowl of soft beef, noodles, and fragrant broth. Whether you favor the clear broth version or the spicy version, it's available in restaurants, night markets, and street vendors around the nation.

Xiao Long Bao

A culinary wonder, these dainty soup dumplings. They are an amazing treat, filled with tasty meat and a blast of aromatic broth. Din Tai Fung is a world-famous restaurant brand that began in Taiwan and is well-known for its Xiao Long Bao.

Gua Bao

Taiwanese pig belly buns, commonly referred to as gua bao, are a wonderful blend of succulent barbecued pork belly, mashed peanuts, and pickled veggies snuggled within a fluffy steamed bun. It is a must-try street dish.

Oyster Omelet

A popular Taiwanese comfort meal, oyster omelets may be discovered at night markets and local cafes. The flavor and texture profile of this dish is created by the mix of plump oysters, scrambled eggs, and sweet potato starch.

Bubble Tea

Bubble tea (or boba tea) originated in Taiwan and has since taken the globe by storm. This refreshing drink mixes the tastes of sweet tea, milk, or fruit with chewy tapioca pearls. It's a refreshing and enjoyable treat that comes in a plethora of flavors and varieties.

Cooking Classes and Food Tours

Ready to advance your passion for Taiwanese food to the next level? Think about taking a cooking class or going on a culinary tour to gain practical expertise and more understanding.

Cooking Lessons

In Taiwan, several cooking institutions and culinary specialists provide lessons where you may learn how to make traditional foods. These lessons are both instructional and delicious, covering everything from rolling your spring rolls to honing the skill of cooking scallion pancakes.

Night Market Food Excursions

Guided food excursions through night markets are a fantastic opportunity to learn about local cuisine while exploring it. Professional guides will show you hidden jewels, explain the history of the cuisine, and assist you in navigating the booths like an experienced eater.

Tea Tasting Tours

Taiwan is well-known for its tea, and you can go on tea-tasting cruises to learn about the differences between oolong, green, and black teas. Tea plantations and traditional tea houses are frequently included on these trips.

Farm-to-Table Activities

Taiwan has a rich agricultural tradition that you may immerse yourself in through farm-to-table activities. Visit nearby farms, choose fresh fruits, and even help with harvesting. It's a fun approach to learning about Taiwan's rural cultures.

CHAPTER 7: TAIWAN'S CULTURAL HERITAGE

Taiwan's cultural past is profoundly embedded in its temples and customs, which depict a fusion of Chinese, indigenous, and other factors.

Temples and Traditions

Longshan Temple

Longshan Temple, one of Taipei's most prominent temples, is a must-see for its exquisite construction and energetic ambiance. It is an assembly of worship and a living testimony to the religious activities of the island. Traditional traditions, which include incense offerings and fortune-telling, may be witnessed.

Chiang Kai-shek Memorial Hall

This landmark Taipei monument honors Taiwan's previous leader, Chiang Kai-shek. The hall is an archaeological site as well as a display of traditional Chinese architecture. The ceremonial replacement of the guard is a serious and spectacular event to see.

Confucius Temples

Taiwan boasts many Confucius temples devoted to the renowned philosopher. These temples serve as hubs of scholarship and the preservation of culture as well as places of devotion. Visiting one gives you an understanding of Confucian philosophy and its effect on Taiwanese civilization.

Traditional Arts

Taiwan has a rich pattern of traditional arts, ranging from puppetry and calligraphy to tea ceremonies and martial arts. Many cultural organizations and museums host exhibitions and courses where you may learn how to do these historical crafts.

Taiwanese Festivals and Celebrations

Taiwanese celebrations are colorful, exuberant, and steeped in cultural traditions.

Lunar New Year

The most significant holiday in Taiwan is the Lunar New Year, frequently referred to as the Spring Festival. Family reunions, temple visits, and the legendary dragon and lion dances are also part of the festivities. For good luck, children and friends are handed red envelopes (hongbao) loaded with money.

Dragon Boat Celebration

This summer celebration features dragon boat racing as well as sticky rice dumplings (zongzi). Rowing teams paddle furiously to the beat of drums, producing an exciting show on Taiwan's rivers and lakes.

Mid-Autumn Festival

This is a moment for moon-watching and eating mooncakes, delectable pastries stuffed with red bean or lotus seed paste. Families come to admire the natural splendor of the full moon.

Ghost Month

The seventh month of the lunar calendar, Ghost Month is a period when Taiwanese people pay homage to their predecessors. To respect the departed, lengthy rituals are done, and many people think that the portals to the underworld are accessible at this time.

Mid-Autumn Festival

The Taiwan Lantern Festival is a beautiful event that features hundreds of multicolored lanterns. The festival is held in an alternate spot each year, exhibiting the culture and customs of that region.

Exploring Taiwan's Indigenous Cultures

Taiwan dwells on a diverse range of ancestral societies, each having its language, customs, and practices.

Atayal and Amis Tribes

The Atayal and Amis tribes are two of Taiwan's major indigenous populations. Traditional dance performances, crafts, and guided explorations of indigenous communities allow you to learn about their traditions.

Paiwan Tribe

The Paiwan inhabitants are well known for their beautiful weaving and tattooing norms, and they provide exceptional cultural interactions. Become familiar with Paiwan's culture and artistic heritage at the Paiwan Cultural Park.

Rukai Tribe

The Rukai are known for their vivid festivals and woodcarving abilities. Attend the yearly Pas-Ta'ai

Festival to see traditional dance performances and art presentations.

Tao Tribe

The Tao tribe lives on Orchid Island, where you may learn about their fishing traditions and practices. The yearly Flying Fish Festival, which celebrates the coming of flying fish, is a feature.

Indigenous Artifacts

Museums such as the National Museum of Prehistory in Taitung and the National Taiwan Museum in Taipei display traditional artifacts, providing a glimpse into the many civilizations that have influenced Taiwan.

CHAPTER 8: EXPERIENCING THE GREAT OUTDOORS

Taiwan's spectacular surroundings make it a hiking and outdoor enthusiast's dream.

Hiking Adventures in Taiwan

Yushan National Park

Taiwan's tallest mountain, Yushan, commonly known as Jade Mountain. It is a difficult yet gratifying journey to reach the highest point. The trail winds past a variety of habitats, from lush woods to alpine tundra, and the view from the summit is spectacular.

Taroko National Park

We've previously seen Taroko Gorge, but the park also has various hiking paths for hikers of all skill levels. Taroko provides possibilities for everyone, whether you want to go for a short walk or a multi-day adventure.

Alishan National Scenic Area

The forests of Alishan are interconnected by hiking paths, each of which offers a distinct adventure. The Giant Tree Trail leads you to magnificent cypress trees that are about 2,000 years old.

Yangmingshan National Park

Yangmingshan, nestled just outside of Taipei, provides a variety of hiking paths across volcanic scenery. The park's hot springs, sulfur vents, and seasonal floral blooms are well-known.

Water Activities: Snorkeling, Surfing, and More

Water sports lovers are going to adore Taiwan's shoreline.

Kenting National Park

Situated in southern Taiwan, Kenting is a popular destination for water sports. The Pacific Ocean's mild waters make it ideal for snorkeling and scuba diving. Investigate coral reefs, colorful aquatic life, and underwater tunnels.

Surfing

The eastern coast of Taiwan, notably in places like Taitung and Hualien, is gaining popularity among surfers. It's a wonderful destination for both amateurs and expert surfers, with steady waves and lovely beaches.

Whale Watching

You may go on whale-watching cruises off the coast of Taiwan to see gorgeous species like humpback whales and spinner dolphins. The whale-watching chances at Penghu and Taitung are well-known.

River Tracing

River tracing, occasionally referred to as canyoning entails trekking, swimming, and, in some cases, rappelling down river gorges. It's a thrilling way to discover Taiwan's inner regions.

Cycling Across Taiwan

Taiwan's cycling lifestyle is thriving, and it's no surprise given the country's well-maintained roads and wonderful surroundings.

Cycling the East Coast Scenic Area

The East Coast Scenic Area provides a natural cycling path along the coast. You'll cycle by rocky cliffs, sandy beaches, and charming fishing communities. It's an excellent approach to appreciating Taiwan's seaside splendor.

Taiwan Cycling Route No. 1

This well-known route surrounds the whole of Taiwan, permitting you to discover Taiwan's various terrains. You'll travel through towns, mountains, and coastal locations, meeting welcoming residents and uncovering hidden treasures along the way.

The Sun Moon Lake Bike Trail

For those looking for an extra leisurely ride, the Sun Moon Lake Bike Trail provides a tranquil riding encounter. The walk around the lake and offers stunning views of the neighboring mountains and temples.

Bicycling in Taroko Gorge

Consider bicycling via Taroko Gorge for a hard yet enjoyable cycling journey. The excursion through the marble cliffs and along the Liwu River is remarkable.

CHAPTER 9: CONNECTING WITH LOCAL

Wow, we've come a long way! Thank you for journeying with me through this guide. I guarantee that this blueprint will take you on a fantastic adventure. To fully enjoy your vacation in Taiwan, it's important to connect with the locals and establish a bond with them. Doing so will enhance your experience and make it even more enjoyable.

Language and Communication Tips

Engaging with people when vacationing in Taiwan may dramatically enhance your trip. To assist you in reconciling any cultural differences, here are some language and communication tips:

Mandarin Chinese

Mandarin is Taiwan's official language and is commonly used. Mastering a few simple words, such as pleasantries and popular gestures, might help you communicate with others. When tourists attempt to speak their language, indigenous people cherish it.

You can get acquainted with the following Mandarin Chinese phrases listed below:

Hello: 你好 (nǐ hǎo)

Goodbye: 再见 (zài jiàn)

Thank you: 谢谢 (xiè xiè)

You're welcome: 不客气 (bù kè qì)

How are you?: 你好吗？ (nǐ hǎo ma?)

I'm fine: 我很好 (wǒ hěn hǎo)

Do you speak English?: 你会说英语吗？ (nǐ huì shuō yīngyǔ ma?)

I don't understand: 我不知道 (wǒ bù zhī dào)

Please: 请 (qǐng)

Thank you very much: 非常感谢 (fēi cháng gǎn xiè)

Sorry: 对不起 (duì bù qǐ)

Taiwanese Hokkien

Aside from Mandarin, a lot of Taiwanese, particularly in the south, speak Taiwanese Hokkien. Being taught a few Hokkien words may be a pleasant way to interact with people and demonstrate your involvement in their ways of life.

Also, below are Taiwanese Hokkien phrases you need to be familiar with:

Hello: 你好！ (nǐ hǎo!)

Goodbye: 再見！(tsài jiàn!)

Thank you: 謝謝！ (tshiah-tsiah!)

You're welcome: 不用客氣！(bô-suì-kheh-khì!)

How are you?: 你好嗎？(nǐ hǎo ma?)

I'm fine: 我很好！(guá hěn hǎo!)

Do you speak English?: 你會講英文嗎？ (nǐ ē-kóng ing-gú ma?)

I don't understand: 我不知道！ (guá m̄-bat-tioh!)

Please: 請！(tshing!)

Thank you very much: 非常謝謝！ (hēng-hēng tshiàh-tsiah!)

Sorry: 對不起！(tui-bû-khì!)

English

While hardly everybody in Taiwan speaks English fluently, particularly in remote environments, younger people and those with jobs in the tourism business can typically interact in English to some level. When in doubt, ask for assistance or guidance.

Translation Applications

To aid communication, look into installing translation applications on your mobile device. Apps like Google Translate may be quite useful for interpreting both written and spoken information.

Body Language

Nonverbal communication, which involves hand motions and expressions on the face may be acknowledged by everyone. Even when language is a limitation, a friendly grin and courteous mannerisms may help establish a sense of connection.

Homestays and Cultural Exchanges

Homestays and cultural exchanges are excellent methods to engage with people and involve oneself in Taiwanese culture:

Homestays

Staying at home with an indigenous family is a wonderful opportunity to enjoy Taiwanese hospitality. You'll get to experience daily living, enjoy meals, and acquire knowledge about the traditions and customs of the area. Homestays may be found across Taiwan, from countryside towns to metropolitan areas.

Cultural Exchange Programs

Cultural exchange programs are offered by multiple institutions and community-based organizations in Taiwan. Traditional tea ceremonies, calligraphy instruction, and hands-on involvement in crafts or cooking can all be part of these events. It's an opportunity to gain knowledge from natives who are enthusiastic about spreading their culture.

Community Events

Maintain your focus on local celebrations and occasions. Being involved in community festivities permits you to meet with locals and learn about their customs directly. These observances, whether a temple procession, a lantern festival, or a village fair, are fantastic chances for exposure to culture.

Language Exchange

Think about getting involved in language exchange organizations or associations. These clubs regularly bring together locals and foreigners who want to learn each other's languages. It's an interactive path where you can practice your language skills while also learning about Taiwanese culture and meeting new people.

Volunteer Opportunities

Volunteering during your time there is an additional opportunity to interact with people. Whether you're assisting with safeguarding the environment, community development, or social problems, you'll have the opportunity to collaborate with Taiwanese people who appreciate your desire to make a difference.

CHAPTER 10: CAPTURING MEMORIES AND FINAL THOUGHT

How has your vacation been so far? Hope you can relate with everything I've exposed in this Guide. It may not be the best blueprint out there, but it's a pocket map to locate Taiwan on your palms.

However, there are a few more things I would love to further discuss to give you a complete package of your memories in Taiwan:

Photography Tips for Taiwan

Photographing the splendor and soul of Taiwan is a pleasant experience. Here are some pointers designed to assist you in capturing unforgettable pictures:

Golden Hours: The sceneries of Taiwan are particularly lovely around the golden hours—early morning and late afternoon. The gentle, glowing light accentuates your subjects' colors and textures.

Landscapes: Use a wide-angle lens to photograph the immensity of sceneries like Taroko Gorge or Sun Moon Lake while capturing Taiwan's various landscapes. To add detail to your photographs, look for fascinating foreground components.

Street Photography: Taiwan's lively suburbs and crowded street markets give good chances for street photography. When photographing close-up photographs, regard people's privacy and request for approval.

Night Photography: When it's dark, Taiwan's cities come alive with brilliant lights and bright signage. Long-exposure photographs of cityscapes should be taken using a tripod. Explore various viewpoints and settings to produce one-of-a-kind photos.

Local Culture: Photograph customary ceremonies, performances, and rites at temples or during holidays to document the spirit of Taiwanese culture. Take note of things such as incense smoke and intricate decorations.

Food Photography: The food scene in Taiwan is an aesthetically pleasing joy. Play with layout and lighting so you can make your food photography as appealing as the meal itself. Remember to photograph the rich colors and textures.

People and Pictures: Take pictures of natives to preserve their personality traits and tales if you interact with them. Always request consent and honor their preferences if they refuse.

Reflections: Taiwan's various bodies of water, such as Sun Moon Lake and the ponds of Alishan, provide an opportunity for magnificent reflection photos. Tranquil lake surfaces can provide mirror-like illusions of the surroundings.

Weather and Seasons: Taiwan has four distinct seasons, each one having its distinct allure. Plan your photographic excursions depending on the weather and the features of the season. For example, cherry blossoms in the spring and blazing leaves in the autumn are ideal subjects for nature photography.

Reflecting on Your Taiwan Journey

When your trip to Taiwan draws to a conclusion, spend a few moments reminiscing on your adventures and memories:

Journaling

Take into account maintaining a travel diary right through the course of your trip. Make a list of your ideas, feelings, and discoveries. Elaborate on the individuals you've met, the locations you've been to, and the tastes you've experienced. It's a lovely way to record your experience and revisit it in the future.

Photograph Albums

Put together your photographs into albums or electronic galleries. Captions and explanations can be added to help you recall the specifics of each experience. Enjoy these albums with your friends and family so you can experience the journey collectively.

Planning Your Next Visit

Taiwan is a place that creates an indelible impact, and you might discover within yourself a yearning for another trip. Here are some suggestions for your subsequent visit:

Explore New Areas: Taiwan boasts a varied range of areas just waiting to be discovered. If you've only explored one portion of the island, try visiting another on your next vacation. Each part of the country has its distinct personality and set of features.

Seasonal Adventures: By the season, Taiwan provides a variety of seasonal activities. Prepare your comeback journey around special events or natural wonders that you haven't witnessed before.

Learn More Mandarin: If you like interacting with natives and wish to improve your communication skills, consider learning deeper Mandarin Chinese. Language abilities can improve your travel memories.

Culinary Quest: Taiwan's culinary terrain is so diverse that you'll never run out of delicacies to sample. Plan a journey centered on cuisine to relish the flavors you skipped on the very first vacation.

Taiwan boasts undiscovered jewels and off-the-beaten-path attractions just waiting to be found. Investigate lesser-known places and schedule a trip off the tourist track.

Extend Your Stay: If you only had a short time on the initial trip, think about staying longer to enjoy yourself even more in Taiwanese culture and everyday life.

Reconnect with Pals: Reunite with any acquaintances you established during your prior visit. Local knowledge may lead to one-of-a-kind experiences and lasting memories.

MY HEART NOTES

As you come to the end of this Taiwan Travel Guide, we sincerely hope that you feel a sense of amazement and motivation. Taiwan is not just a place to visit; it's a captivating blend of culture, nature, and warm hospitality that has made an everlasting impression on your trip.

In this book, we have gone on an incredible journey, exploring the lively streets of Taipei and the peaceful scenery of Taroko Gorge. We've also indulged in delicious street food and delved into Taiwan's diverse cultural legacy. Throughout our travels, Taiwan has welcomed us with open arms, unveiling its various aspects and encouraging us to discover, encounter, and appreciate its true nature.

When you think back on your time in Taiwan, remember the sincere smiles and infectious laughter of the locals you met, the delectable flavors that tantalized your taste buds, and the awe-inspiring landscapes that left you speechless. These memories will always have a special place in your travel story, reminding you of the wonderful experiences you had.

Taiwan is a remarkable island that boasts stunning and picturesque nature. However, your journey does not end here. Taiwan will leave a lasting imprint on your soul, calling you back to explore more and delve deeper into its treasures. You can hike to new heights, dive into crystal-clear waters, or indulge in culinary delights. There is always more to discover on this enchanting island.

There is always more to explore on this captivating island. Taiwan is a destination that offers boundless opportunities for discovery. As you finish reading this book, cherish the memories you've created in your heart. Let them motivate you to embark on your next adventure, whether it's a return to this island haven or an exploration of another part of the globe. Remember, travel is not just about the journey, but also about the experiences and memories that last a lifetime.

Thank you for allowing us to be a part of your Taiwan journey. May your travels continue to be filled with curiosity, joy, and the magic of discovery. Until we meet again on the road, may your next adventure be as unforgettable as the heart of Taiwan itself. Safe travels and zaijian (再见), until we meet again!

Adeline Palmerstone

Made in United States
Troutdale, OR
10/06/2024